GETTING THE
LITTLE
BLIGHTERS
TO EAT

Change your children from fussy eaters into foodies

CLAIRE POTTER

Illustrated by Mark Beech

FEATHERSTONE
AN IMPRINT OF BLOOMSBURY
LONDON NEW DELHI NEW YORK SYDNEY

To Molly and Mike, the original little blighters
(I still haven't told mum you fed most of
your dinner to the dog under the table)

Published 2013 by Featherstone Education
an imprint of Bloomsbury Publishing Plc
50 Bedford Square, London WC1B 3DP

www.bloomsbury.com

Bloomsbury is a registered trademark of Bloomsbury Publishing Plc

Text © Claire Potter 2013
Illustrations © Mark Beech 2013

A CIP catalogue for this book is available from the British Library.

All rights reserved. No part of this publication may be reproduced in any
form or by any means – graphic, electronic, or mechanical, including
photocopying, recording, taping or information storage and retrieval
systems – without the prior permission in writing of the publishers.

ISBN 978-1-4081-9074-6

MIX
Paper from
responsible sources
FSC
www.fsc.org   FSC® C013604

Printed and bound by CPI Group (UK) Ltd, Croydon, CR0 4YY

10

To see our full range of titles visit www.bloomsbury.com

THE RULES

FOREWORD

Fussy eating among children is a widespread problem in the UK. At last count, it accounted for nearly 50% of our general clinic referrals and when we see them the parents are often desperate and at their wits ends.

When Claire first approached me to provide specialist support for her book, I was initially cautious. Fussy eating is not something that will disappear overnight, simply as it does not develop overnight. Altering these behaviours is a challenge and involves commitment and consistency from the parents, as well as honest reflection regarding household traits.

I have had many parents tell me about books and articles they have read which were unhelpful, either because they were complicated and difficult to understand or because they made them feel like a failure. However, during our first chat it became apparent that this book was something I'd like to be involved in. The approach and ideas were refreshing to hear as they entirely matched what we recommend in the clinic. In addition, the presentation and tone was light, easy to read, practical, friendly and supportive with the simple format of 'rules' to follow.

The ethos behind the book is one I fully support. Fussy eating is often discussed as though it is a milestone of childhood: something that every child will develop at some point. Yet – with the exception of some children with specific learning needs – I do not believe this is the case. Fussy eating is a combination of a child's developing independence and control and the parents' reaction to it. With parents' positive management of the situation it does not need to develop into a persistent problem and behaviours can be changed so that children are eating a greatly improved and varied diet – and most importantly, enjoying it. Food is not only a physiological requirement to nourish the body but also a time for families to converse with one another and experience new tastes, textures, smells and sensations.

If your ambition is to create positive, stress-free and happy mealtimes that no-one dreads or fears, then this book is a great place to begin. Remember though, that to achieve significant change, the advice needs to be followed consistently, day in, day out!

Anna Groom
Registered Dietitian, ASD
NHS Specialist Paediatric Dietitian

INTRODUCTION

One of my most vivid childhood memories is a Sunday afternoon when I was six years old. We'd just had a roast dinner. My parents had gone into the living room to watch a film, but I'd stayed in the kitchen with my sister, then two years old, who was still strapped in her highchair – having been told that she would stay there until she had finished all her food. It felt too cruel to leave her. She wasn't crying. She'd gone past that. She just looked utterly broken.

The details are still imprinted on my brain: the cold, brown mush in her Peter Rabbit bowl, her terry towelling bib with light blue trim, the square, wooden highchair, the 1970s' plastic, orange clock on the wall, ticking loudly against the sad, intense silence. I offered her a spoonful but she didn't respond or even change her expression.

Suddenly, with an explosion of courage, my heart thumping, terrified of being caught, I grabbed her bowl, dashed out the back door, scraped the food into the dustbin, rushed back in, placed the bowl on the highchair tray and shouted triumphantly, 'Mum...Dad...She's finished!' My mum came into the kitchen, looked at the empty bowl with surprise and puzzlement, but took my sister out of her highchair. The relief I felt was enormous. I'd rescued her. Crisis over.

I don't want you to think for one moment that my parents were tyrants. They were simply at the end of their tether with my sister's fussy eating and acutely worried that she wasn't getting enough nutrients. Under that strain, on that particular day, they had resorted to an authoritarian stance that wasn't that uncommon in those days: an if-you-don't-eat-it-now-you'll-have-it-for-breakfast type of approach!

Although this incident stands out in my mind, over the years I accumulated many more memories of tensions and battles around the dinner table – right down to small details like being told off for making faces in my mousse before I ate it! When I look back, I have to say I remember mealtimes with a heavy heart.

Consequently, when I had my own children, I was determined to make the dinner table a happy place. I wanted food and eating to be only a positive thing. I didn't want tension, negotiations, arguments, orders, punishments or tears – and I didn't want fussiness. They felt interconnected to me. If all the emphasis was on the enjoyment of food, wouldn't my children be less fussy?

A basic plan formed in my mind. It wasn't an obvious or intuitive one, or even based on common sense. In fact, in many ways, it went against a parent's natural instincts. I put it into place from the day I weaned my first child – and kept going. Fourteen years later, I have a teenage son who has always eaten absolutely everything except raw tomato, and a seven-year-old daughter who is very happy with whatever comes her way, but never touches beetroot! They are both full of interest in and enthusiasm for food. In every other way, they are completely different personalities, and I know their non-fussiness can't be genetic because my daughter is adopted.

However, what I needed to know was whether my approach would work not just to prevent fussy eating, but to 'cure' fussy eating – to reverse the situation with children who were already fussy. I consulted NHS Specialist Paediatric Dietitian Anna Groom who works with fussy eating children of all ages. In many of her cases, the problem has become extreme. My approach, she said, formed the bedrock of the way she worked with the parents of these children to successfully reduce their fussiness. We went on to discuss my approach at length and in detail to test it against her expertise, experience and knowledge of the latest research. Finally, it was boiled down to the list of 30 Rules that are contained in this book.

When people ask me how I made my children non-fussy eaters, I often joke that I have rigged up my dinner table to deliver a system of electric shocks! In fact, the very opposite is true. The approach is very human, non-punitive and non-confrontational. It's not about making children non-fussy. It's about setting up the conditions which encourage and develop a positive, relaxed and open-minded attitude to food; conditions in which fussiness becomes irrelevant.

Wishing you a future of fuss-free family meals!

Claire Potter

RULE NO. 1

Don't tell yourself that children are just naturally fussy

It's easy to resign ourselves to the idea that children are fussy eaters by nature. To think that it's the norm. To decide that there's very little we can do. We meet and talk to so many other parents with the same problem that we can't help but think that it's just how children are. All we can do for now is grin and bear it and hope they'll grow out of it.

Our children may or may not grow out of it (there are plenty of fussy eating adults!) but in the meantime it's still incredibly important that they have a nutritious, varied diet. After all, they're still growing and developing. Their cells are still multiplying. Their bones, their brains, their everything, are not just being fed – they're still being made!

That aside, wouldn't it be fantastic to have mealtimes that were always fuss-free, stress-free and enjoyable? To have happy, positive, relaxed children at the table – whatever you're serving?

The good news is you do have the power to change things. And quite quickly too – we're talking a matter of months, not years.

Many parents say that their children weren't fussy as babies: they gobbled down the puréed carrot, ate the mushed up cauliflower cheese and generally seemed to enjoy whatever came their way. They say their children started to become fussy when they were two or three years old. Why does it happen at this age? Because it is at this point that children catch onto the fact that we really, really care about what they eat and that fussy eating is going to get them a lot of attention.

It doesn't matter if the attention is negative: *Come on, you've hardly touched your mashed potato...You're not having any pudding if you don't eat your dinner...Why have you left your peas?* Our children crave attention from us! On top of that, it's usually around toddlerdom that they twig that being fussy will give them an awful lot of power (but more on that a bit later).

Of course most children and adults will have one or two foods that they are instinctively averse to. I have an uneasy relationship with oranges for example! But these foods aside, you really can reverse fussiness and have children who pretty much tuck into whatever's offered to them.

Boy! Am I gonna be a fussy eater!

So forget the idea that fussy eating is a compulsory part of childhood! Instead, make a pact with yourself that you will do everything you can to overcome the problem.

The research

Studies on the eating habits of identical and non-identical twins between seven and 11 years old suggest that genes can partly influence which foods a child prefers and which foods they might be cautious about. However, it was found that environmental factors play a significant part and can actually override any genetic programming. The parent's reaction and behaviour around food determines how far it goes and whether it becomes a fussy eating problem.

The paediatric dietitian says...

'My experience tells me that children are not naturally fussy – but they will become so if the conditions are right! Follow the rules in this book consistently and you should start to see a little progress after two weeks, and a lot after three or four months.'

RULE NO. 2

Forget everything your mother (or grandmother) told you!

You're going to sit, there until you've eaten it.

Think of all the starving children...

Finish, that last bit. It's not good to waste food.

You won't grow big and, strong if you don't eat your vegetables.

Did your parents or grandparents say these kinds of things to you? Do you ever hear something similar coming out of your own mouth?

Often, the things we do and say to our children around food are inherited from the generations before us. We may copy their approach on purpose because it seems like conventional wisdom or common sense. Or we may have absorbed it by osmosis and do it automatically and unthinkingly. Or it may be something we try not to do but revert to when we're at the end of our tether! Of course, just because our parents or grandparents did something, it doesn't necessarily make it right.

It's never a good idea to copy the way our parents did things unless we have first thought it through ourselves and decided it is the best way.

Is there a good reason for it? Is it effective? Is it really a good approach? The *well, it didn't do me any harm* way of thinking might be harmful – or at least very unhelpful – in the fight against fussy eating.

These kind of comments were generally rooted in the wartime and post-wartime periods when food was rationed and there was less variety available: an egg was precious if you only got one a week. You couldn't turn your nose up at a tin of spam if that's all there was in the larder for dinner that day. You couldn't reject vegetables from the garden if they were the only vegetables to be had. It was important not to waste any food and to eat everything you were given to get the nutrition you needed.

But this kind of approach just isn't relevant today and it certainly won't encourage your child to eat something! It will only create negativity, tension, battlegrounds and unhappiness at the dinner table. As you will see, it is entirely at odds with what the rules in this book recommend.

So throw everything of this sort that anyone ever said to you as a child out of the window and start afresh. And if you hear something along these lines about to come out of your mouth, stop yourself!

The paediatric dietitian says...

'As a parent you will get a lot of different advice, but be selective about what you choose to follow. Times have changed. Tackling fussy eating may mean a few teaspoons worth of wasted food, but the emphasis should be on the enjoyment of food.'

RULE NO. 3

Don't label your child a fussy eater

As a child I was extremely shy. I never initiated conversation with another child and if an adult asked me a question, I would hold my head down coyly and stay silent. *Ahh, is she shy?* they'd ask. *Yes* my mum or dad would say. *She's really shy.* The effect of this? I thought of myself as a 'shy child'. It became my identity. I lived up to it, perpetuated it and used it as an excuse for not taking part in things. It took me a long, long time to break out of that mould and I missed out on a lot of opportunities along the way.

It is well researched that labelling children with anything – positive or negative (*very sporty, naughty boy, artistic, not good at reading*) – becomes a self-fulfilling prophecy. Children internalize the label they are given. In general, if the label is positive and full of expectation, they do well in that area of life. If the label is negative and they are not expected to succeed, they do badly.

Never tell your child they're a fussy eater – or let them hear you telling anyone else! If you do, they are more likely to continue to conform to that label. Subconsciously they will be thinking: *No one is expecting me to eat this. I'm a fussy eater. I can't help it.*

She's Little Miss Fussy!

It will make it much harder to overcome the problem. Be careful too about comparing your children. Don't let them hear you say things like *He's easy...he'll eat anything... but this one...she's a nightmare!* This polarises your children at opposite ends of the spectrum and encourages them to stay there – or go even further in that direction. The fussy one could get fussier!

By all means, discuss their fussy eating habits and what they will and won't eat when they're not there, but never in front of them.

The science

From about the age of three to nine, children's brainwaves look like the brainwaves of an adult under hypnosis. So when you say something to a child in that age range, it is instantly absorbed and accepted as 'the truth' without question. The purpose of this is that it allows children to learn huge quantities of information easily. The downside is that they can whole-heartedly absorb attitudes and values – including beliefs about themselves – which may be detrimental!

The paediatric dietitian says...

'Be really careful not to talk about your child's fussy eating at all when they're around – not even in whispers or behind your hand!'

RULE NO. 4

Give up your power!

Children have very little power in their lives. We make them do their homework, clean their room, put their shoes on. We decide what time they go to bed, what they wear, when they watch TV… And even if we do give them a say in some of this stuff, we still, in the end, have the final say. That's the downside of being a child. You have to wait until you're a grown-up before you can live your life exactly how you want to!

So, what's this got to do with fussy eating? Eating is the one area where children soon learn that it's easy for them to have a lot of power: superpower in fact!

By rejecting certain foods or insisting on others they can control us emotionally and physically. One *Yuck!* could make us cross. A barely touched meal could make us worried or upset. They might even be able to get us running around like an eager-to-please chef, cooking to their orders or making them a different meal from everyone else in the family. Perhaps they can get us to cut off their egg white or pick out all the bits of onion from their bolognese sauce. One way or another, fussy eating – finally – puts them in charge!

Take this example of a mother and her chubby-cheeked two-year-old boy. He'd become very fussy and she was worried he wasn't eating enough. As she put a bowl of tuna and sweetcorn pasta in front of him, she said, *Now, I want you to eat your lunch today.* Did he? He had one spoonful. The mother cajoled him, pleaded with him, threatened him, told him off and was eventually almost in tears. *See?* she said desperately. Her son, meanwhile, had the most mischievous twinkle in his eyes: an air of smug satisfaction. He was the boss! It wasn't that he didn't like the food. It wasn't that he wasn't hungry. He was just having so much fun exerting his power over his mother – and getting so much attention for it. Afterwards, as he went off to play, she gave him a piece of bread as he'd barely eaten. Child: 100 points. Mother: 0.

Don't invite children to a power battle in the first place. When it comes to eating, behave as if you have no power. Completely let go of the parent-to-child authority that you use in other areas of life. Just simply give your child their food and act as if you don't mind whether they eat it or not.

No commands, no orders, no tellings off, no threats, no punishments, no bribes. We will cover the ins and outs of this in other rules, but for now, keep this basic approach in mind.

It may sound risky, even scary (*But then they might not eat anything!*) but it will soon start to pay off. It takes away all a child's power over you around food and puts you in a much better position – because if there's no battle for them to try and 'win' you'll have so much more chance of them eating what you hope they'll eat.

How many days would it have taken of just giving this boy his lunch to reverse the situation? Maybe two or three. Four maximum. It wouldn't take long for him to realise there was much more pleasure to be got from eating his lunch if there was no power or attention to be gained from not eating it.

The paediatric dietitian says...

'I don't think fussy eating is actually about food at all in the first instance. Children quickly learn that food is the easiest area for them to get control, as well as lots of attention. They will soon forget about 'the power struggle' surrounding eating if you remove it.'

RULE NO. 5

Stay in control of the shopping and cooking

A mother in a supermarket asked her four-year old boy, *What do you want for tea tonight? Pizza*, he replied. *No, I'm not buying you pizza. I gave you pizza the other night and you didn't eat it…what about pasta…or…?* *No*, said the boy adamantly. *I want pizza.* And so the argument continued.

The previous rule told you to relinquish your power as a parent over your child's eating. However, the one area where you should and must keep control is in the food shopping and the cooking. Before the food gets to the table, you are the boss!

You decide what to serve. They decide whether to eat it or not. **Present a variety of meals regardless of your child's reaction – the ones they love, the ones they quite like and the ones they turn their noses up at! No choices. No alternatives. No extra snacks to compensate.**

If you let your child dictate what you buy and cook, you will be falling down at the first hurdle. You'll have no chance of expanding their diet. You'll be nurturing fussy eating. You must buy and cook what you want to, not what *they* want you to.

So when you're in the supermarket, don't ask them what they fancy for dinner or if they'd prefer spaghetti or rice tonight. Don't be pestered into buying white bread if you'd really rather buy brown bread. Don't be bullied into buying cheese strings if they weren't on your list. You're in charge.

The same goes in the kitchen. Don't look in your food cupboards, fridge or freezer and say *What do you want for dinner tonight?* or *Would you prefer X or Y?* Don't prepare different meals for different family members and never jump up and make them another meal or give them something else if they don't eat what's on offer. If they complain about what you're giving them, avoid any harsh or negative responses like *Well, if you don't eat this, you're not getting anything else.* Just say gently and calmly, *This is what we're having today.*

Remember, once the meal is served, give up your power. Now it's up to them.

A word on snacks

Make sure you're in control of snacks too – both what and when! Left to their own devices, many children would happily graze through the day. There can be a temptation to withhold snacks, thinking it will make your child more likely to eat their lunch or dinner, but letting them get voraciously hungry and irritable isn't going to be a good lead up to mealtimes. Give children a snack mid-morning and mid-afternoon to keep their mood even. It would be reasonable to offer a choice if it's no trouble, but limit it to two things (eg. *banana* or *toast*).

The paediatric dietitian says...

'When it comes to food shopping and cooking, you don't need to try and be your child's friend. It is reasonable to let your child choose a meal occasionally as a treat, but not more than once a week.'

15

RULE NO. 6

Don't use pudding as a reward or punishment

> If you eat all your lunch up, you can have a chocolate mousse afterwards.

> You're not getting any pudding unless you eat a bit more.

> Finish your beans and you can have a piece of that cake.

How many times have you heard yourself say something along these lines? They are words that trip so easily off the tongue.

It may feel like the obvious, common sense thing to do: if they eat the nutritious, savoury bit, then they are allowed to have the sweet, rubbishy bit. Surely, it's an effective way to encourage children to eat? No. Dangling pudding in front of your child in this way actually does more harm than good.

The message it gives is this: the main course is not that enjoyable. Eating it is a chore. But it's something you just have to endure to get to the pudding – which is the delicious bit and the bit worth getting to.

The message may be sub-conscious but it's loud and clear and we are reinforcing it every time we use pudding as a reward or punishment.

The actual truth is that both savoury and sweet food is nice. But in general, the savoury food is much healthier and tends to be the part children fuss over, so we certainly don't want to convey any negative messages about it.

Second of all, the dinner table is not the place for punishments. We want only positive associations with mealtimes and a convivial atmosphere.

Withholding pudding could cause resentment, anger, arguments or tears.

So what should you do if your child hasn't eaten much of their main course or the part of their meal that you particularly wanted them to eat? Give them a little pudding anyway, ideally something simple like fruit or yoghurt. But refrain from saying, *You didn't eat X so you can only have fruit or yoghurt today* because that sounds like a punishment too!

It's actually better, anyway, if pudding – other than fruit – is an occasional rather than an everyday thing. If your child gets used to always finishing their meal on a sweet note, their body will get conditioned to wanting, expecting and anticipating that – which will encourage them to bypass their main course if it isn't one of their favourites.

The paediatric dietitian says...

'Even if telling them to eat their dinner to get pudding works, it is never a good idea. It teaches them to ignore their feelings of fullness - they might overeat to get pudding, and then they have pudding as well!'

Don't push them to eat everything on their plate

Have you ever been served a big plate of food and thought: *Crikey, I'll never eat all that!* Did you feel a bit overwhelmed? Did you feel under pressure? Did you struggle? Did it make the food less rather than more appealing?

At first glance, teaching our children that the aim is to eat all of their breakfast/lunch/dinner seems like a reasonable thing to do. We want their tummies to be full. We don't want food wasted. But it's actually a big no-no.

How do we know how big our child's meals should be? It's just guesswork. To put an arbitrary amount of food on their plate and expect them to eat all of it just isn't logical. Maybe the portion is just too big and they're getting negative feedback from us for leaving food on their plate when they've actually eaten plenty.

And don't you have days, or certain times of the day, when you're hungrier than others? So do children, of course.

Let your child decide the amount they eat. The motto should be 'Eat as much or as little as you like'.

Once the pressure of being expected to eat it all – or a certain amount – is taken away, the mood will be lighter and more laid-back. We'll be giving our children the message that food is enjoyable – not a chore or an endurance test. And very importantly, we won't be inviting them to yet another battle of wills! It may take a little while, but they really will start to eat more of what we want them to eat, not less.

Apart from the positive effect this approach will have on fussy eating, it will allow them to listen to their bodies and eat the right amount. After all, the natural and healthy thing to do is to eat until you are comfortably full – not more or less. You shouldn't feel stuffed or hungry at the end of a meal. We don't want our children to grow up conditioned to think they should always eat everything on their plate, whatever the quantity. It's a bad habit to take into adulthood and could lead to obesity.

Watch out in cafés and restaurants too. Children's meals are often too large and set up very unrealistic expectations about portion size.

You haven't eaten much we might say disapprovingly, when actually they have!

Their hunger, not the amount of food on their plate, should always determine how much they eat.

A word on waste

But what about all the food that's going to be wasted, you might say? It can't be a good thing to teach children that it's okay to waste food! The best way to minimise waste is to offer a smaller meal first and allow for seconds. Any leftovers can then usually be kept and eaten at another time or incorporated into another meal. It can be very overwhelming for children to be faced with a big meal anyway. Start small, go bigger!

The paediatric dietitian says...

'Fussy eaters are very rarely underweight. They generally eat enough of the foods they like and meet their calorie requirements. It's usually only the parent's perception that they're not eating enough. If you put everything they ate in a day on a plate, you might be surprised.'

19

Don't tell them to eat anything – let alone make them!

> I want you to have a bit more of the shepherd's pie.

> Look, you haven't touched your rice. Eat some of it at least.

> Try just one Brussels sprout for me – please?

> Don't forget your carrots. They help you see in the dark you know.

We want our children to eat lots of different foods. We want them to eat enough. The obvious thing to do then is to tell them to, right? Encourage them. Remind them. Ask them nicely. Give them a little nudge in the right direction…or a big push! Not at all.

Telling children to eat something is just another way of showing them how much we care. We're offering attention for not eating something and inviting them to battle it out with us. It puts them firmly in the driving seat.

We actually have more – not less – chance of them eating what we want them to eat if we *don't* tell them to.

> Eat your broccoli.

Remember the basic principles: we simply provide the food. They choose whether to eat it – and how much.

Telling them to eat this or eat that, can also come across as nagging and make the table a less happy, relaxed place to be. Of course, if they're used to us telling them what to eat, once we stop, they aren't going to suddenly devour those foods. But give it a little time. Saying nothing will be much more effective.

At the same time, we should avoid discussing at the dinner table with our child why they should eat something. *Fish is good for your brain...You need the potatoes for energy... Peppers are full of vitamin C.* Children absolutely should learn about healthy eating and the different food groups and nutrients that their body needs – but the dinner table is not the time for a lesson. They are very unlikely to be receptive to it when they are 'in the moment' of that meal. It only adds to the pressure and gives them more to rebel against. Would you want a lesson on why getting a good night's sleep is important when you're settling down to sleep? Do talk to your children about healthy eating, but do it away from the table.

Finally, never, ever make your child eat something. Don't force them to sit at the table until they've eaten it, for example, or spoon feed them food they don't want.

Never use dominance or restraint in any way. That'll make the table a very unhappy place and could create some very deep, long-term issues around food.

The research

One study interviewed over 100 college students about being made or forced to eat food as children. One of the most common tactics was being made to sit at the table until they'd eaten it. When asked if they now ate the food they were made to eat, 72% said they didn't. The conclusion was that when a child finally gives in and eats something he doesn't want to, he perceives himself the 'loser' and the parent the 'winner'. So later in life, when it's up to him, he usually chooses to 'win' and not eat the food.

The paediatric dietitian says...

'There needs to be trust around food. Making a child eat something causes tears and tantrums and sets up such negative associations with eating. This can create a much bigger problem. You'll have success much more quickly if you don't do this.'

21

85% healthy

RULE NO. 9

Keep their diet as savoury as possible

A couple were having lunch in a café with their two daughters, about two and four years old. The mum was having a chicken tikka baguette and a cup of tea and the father was having soup and bread. The children both had two slices of white toast with strawberry jam and hot chocolate. They were chatting and laughing and got very distracted at one point. *Eat your lunch*...said the father gently...*or you won't get your sweets this afternoon.* In other words: eat this sugary sweet stuff and you can have more sugary sweet stuff!

You can be sure the more sugar you give a child, the more they'll want. It really does grease the slippery slope to fussy eating and makes it much harder to reverse it. I'm not advocating that we should never give our children sweets or chocolate or a slice of cake – that'll only turn sweet stuff into elusive manna from heaven in their eyes! But aim to keep the bulk of their diet savoury.

If you feed the body lots of nutritious, savoury stuff, it gets conditioned to wanting more of that. It sends messages to your brain that tell you what your body needs. As a result, you want a variety of foods and fancy the right things to eat. But if you feed the body lots of sugar, it thinks, *Wow, this is heaven…I want more!* Eating sugar is highly pleasurable, momentarily blissful even. It's addictive. When the body has a sugar hit, it's very difficult to ignore or fight the powerful cravings for more sugar. Sugar makes you lose touch with what your body really wants and needs. Cucumber or spinach just aren't going to look that enticing!

If your child has lots of sweet foods, aim to re-adjust their diet so that 80-90% of it is savoury.

It will gradually re-programme them to have more of a taste and appetite for nutritious foods.

Sweet, sugary foods are, after all, empty calories that leave little space or hunger for more nutritious food. It can help to think of your child's young, growing body as a clean, glass, see-through vessel you're filling up each day with good things that'll help them grow and thrive.

The science

Sugar is absorbed very quickly by the body and triggers the release of serotonin, a chemical that makes us feel happy. The pancreas manages the sudden rise in blood sugar level by producing a large amount of insulin. This causes your blood sugar level to drop quickly which makes us feel fatigued and low. In order to restore blood sugar levels to normal and get another 'high', your brain creates strong signals urging you to eat more sugary food – even when you're not hungry!

TIPS: Stick to a once-a-week 'Sweets day' (see page 46).

- Don't always have pudding or end meals on a sweet note.
- Give children peanut butter, yeast extract, cream cheese or something else savoury on toast and in sandwiches – not jam, treacle or chocolate spread.
- Don't buy sugar-coated cereals like frosted flakes or chocolate-flavoured ones. Stick to regular cornflakes, plain wheat-based cereals, instant oats or porridge.
- Give children a savoury snack like a cracker with cheese, rather than reaching for a biscuit or chocolate bar – even if it's a bit more trouble to prepare.
- Offer a bread roll as a snack when you're in the supermarket (see page 47).
- If there's a choice of plain or sweet (e.g. rice cakes, popcorn) buy the plain.
- Don't have a 'goodies cupboard' or tin in your house full of sweets and chocolate that your child will constantly hanker after!

The paediatric dietitian says...

'No food should be disallowed or called 'bad', but everything should be eaten in the appropriate quantity. There are a lot of calories in sugar – and nothing else!'

RULE NO. 10

Keep offering them the foods they don't eat

> We love fish pie, but I always make the children something different because I know they won't touch it.

> I hate the idea of him going hungry.

> I don't bother buying it anymore – they don't eat it.

> I used to make chilli every week but she started picking at it and it drove me nuts.

Putting food on our child's plate that we know from past experience they almost certainly won't eat does feel like a waste of time, a waste of effort, a waste of money and a waste of food. Why bother?

Research shows that it can take children 15–20 times of being offered a food before they will be receptive to the idea of eating it.

If we don't put it on their plate in the first place, we will be taking away the opportunity to ever reach that point. If we don't at least expose them to it, it will be impossible to increase the number of different foods they eat.

> Here we go again! The 17th time!

24

So just because your child has turned their nose up at a food once or twice – or even ten times! – don't stop presenting them with it. If they seem to have gone off sausages and gravy recently, don't take them off the menu. If your child never touches runner beans, still put a few on their plate. If the only fruit they've eaten for months are oranges and bananas, don't stop giving them other fruit. Offer, offer, offer!

There's no need to be mathematical about it with charts and tick boxes to count the number of times you've offered a food – and then stop if they're still rejecting it after the twentieth time! Just plan, cook and dish up family meals with no regard for who has and hasn't eaten what in the past. Matter-of-factly present the food without putting any pressure on children to eat it. If they question why it's on their plate, remind them that they only have to eat what they want to. And to avoid lots of food wasteage, just put a very small amount on their plate in the first instance.

It's all about exposure and opportunity. It may take time for them to come round to the idea of eating a food they've previously rejected but keep going. And even if one day they do eat it, don't automatically assume they'll eat it the next time, or every single time after that. Be patient. Gradually you will see a permanent difference.

The research

There have been many studies in this area, but one study took 360 nine and ten-year olds and offered them tiny servings of carrot, peas, tomato and pepper once a week for ten weeks. There was no pressure to eat them – the children were allowed to spit the vegetables out into a napkin or not taste them at all if they wished. It took a minimum of six tasting sessions to observe any change in their liking, and eight or nine times for children to say they liked a vegetable they had previously said they disliked.

The paediatric dietitian says...

'Exposure to food is a really important first step in building children's trust and confidence in their ability to experience new foods. We need to get them used to having it on their plate regardless of whether they eat it or not. When I work with children who are phobic about a particular food, I get them to draw it, touch it, play with it, smell it, kiss it, lick it!'

RULE NO. 11

Don't buy into the idea of 'children's food'

I recently saw a TV advert for a new range of children's meals available in the supermarket. The slogan was something like: *Meals to get them eating just like you!* Eh? I thought. So, let me get this straight. They were suggesting that I bought special meals for my children – while I presumably ate a different meal – so that they would be eating just like me. What kind of twisted thinking (or clever, double-bluff marketing) was that? How about I just give them what I'm eating instead? That sounds like a better, quicker, easier and cheaper way to achieve the same thing!

There are whole shelves in supermarkets dedicated to 'children's food', but it's all just gimmicks: turkey dinosaurs, soups for kids, tinned Tommy Tiger pasta shapes, packets of children's rice, toddler's bangers and mash meals, breaded fish in the shape of fish, packs of children's bananas. (Bananas! How are they different from any other bananas once they're out of the packaging with the fun characters on?)

The line between 'children's food' and 'adults' food' is imaginary. It's invented.

These foods may be flavoured or shaped differently, or packaged powerfully to try and make you – and your child – think you should buy them. That you'll have more chance of your child eating them than other foods. Or even that they're healthier for your child in some way.

But buying these types of foods simply encourages fussy eating. It puts the idea into our and our children's heads that they shouldn't – or can't – eat the same food as adults. That they should stay within certain boundaries. That they have 'special' food needs and desires that parents should cater to. Boiled carrots probably aren't going to interest you that much if you've got used to being given carrot from a squeezy pouch!

Even if we avoid these very gimmicky foods, we may assume that our children won't eat what we eat and put them on a 'child-friendly' diet – you know, fish fingers, chicken nuggets, sausages, chips, pizza, plain pasta – while we eat more interesting, colourful meals.

It is much, much better to give our children exactly the same food that

we are eating. We may not always be able to eat dinner at the same time as them, because of work or other commitments, but we should aim to cook one meal for everybody as often as possible – even if we have to save ours to eat later or save some for our children to have the next day.

The paediatric dietitian says...

'Experience has shown me that bringing up children on home-cooked food, shared with the adults in the family, definitely results in less fussy eating and an acceptance of a wider range of tastes and textures.'

Eating out

When you go to a café or restaurant, there will often be a Children's menu full of 'safe' options like sausage, chicken nuggets or burger with chips. Instead, try asking if they'll do a half-portion of an adult meal for half the price – and let your child choose freely. It can make your child feel privileged and grown-up and encourages adventurousness. Until the age of three or even older – depending on their appetite – you can just ask for an empty plate and give them bits of everything from your (and your partner's) plate. A child's meal portion is often too large for a two or three year old anyway. This will expose them to a much wider variety of food.

RULE NO. 12

Don't give a running commentary at mealtimes

Imagine this. You're eating dinner. It's roast lamb with all the trimmings, one of your favourites. Your partner is eating too but is watching you. As you put a mouthful of roast potato into your mouth, he says, *I bet you're enjoying that potato! They're lovely and crispy, aren't they?* You nod your head. You cut a piece of lamb and eat it with some mint sauce. Your partner says, *I think the meat's your favourite bit. There's lots of protein in that, you know.* You ignore him this time. You're just about to take a forkful of carrots, when he says, *Try the carrots. They're cooked beautifully.* Grrrr. Leave me alone, you think. You have another potato instead.

You get the drift. Having someone constantly commenting on what you're eating or not eating – even in the most gentle and positive way – would drive you nuts! It would make you want to not eat. Yet many of us do this to our children all the time!

A mother in a café had just bought her two-year-old son a meal of sausage, chips and baked beans. The child looked very pleased. The mother had the best will in the world: *Do you like sausage?...Yes you doooo!...Where's that sausage gone?...It's in your tummy!...Ooh, you're going to have a chip now...Is it yummy?...You love the tomato sauce, don't you...Let me put a few beans on the spoon for you...How about another piece of sausage? You like sausage...* It didn't matter that her voice was light and playful and encouraging. She may as well have been screaming *EAT IT! EAT IT! EAT IT! I really want you to eat it.*

About a fifth of a way through the meal, the child pushed his plate away.

Not only is this kind of commentary annoying, it gives your child incredible power again. If I don't eat this, or that, thinks the child, it will really bother them and I'll get more attention.

Give your child their food and then say nothing about it. Talk about other stuff instead. Don't watch and monitor their every mouthful like a hawk either – or at least don't let them see you doing this!

This way, your child really is more likely, not less likely, to eat what you hope they'll eat!

The school lunch interrogation

This rule also applies to other times when you're not there. Do you rummage through your children's lunchbox after school and comment on what they have and haven't eaten? Or do you quiz your child about hot school dinners? What was it today? Did you like it? Did you eat it all? Stop! It won't change the past and it could make things worse.

The paediatric dietitian says...

'Focus on the conversation, not the food. Constantly referring to the food at mealtimes creates pressure and gives your child something to react against.'

RULE NO. 13

Keep introducing them to new and unfamiliar foods

Why is the moon sometimes out in the daytime? How far can dogs smell? What does it feel like if you touch an electric fence? What's wrong with that man's legs? Children are naturally curious and inquisitive. They ask endless random questions as they try to figure out the world. This interest in new things does naturally include food too and is very evident when they're very little – they want to try the mustard on the table, they want to eat an anchovy off your pizza, they want a sip of your beer... they are open to it all and have built up no preconceptions about what's nice and not nice to eat.

But it's so easy for us to accidentally knock this adventurous spirit out of them with the things we do and say to them around food. Before we know it, their *Ooh, what's that?* approach to foods they haven't seen or tasted before has turned to a *Ergh, I'm not even going to try that* attitude.

This can make us nervous or even scared of presenting them with new foods, but if we want to reverse their incredible shrinking palate, we have to keep doing it.

The first step, as we said before, is exposure – seeing, smelling, touching a food. If we don't at least give them the opportunity to try new foods, how can they? We have no chance of opening their minds – let alone their palates – to new tastes, flavours and textures.

At first, make gradual and tiny changes to your food shopping. Tweak by little tweak. As you put a food item into your basket, stop and ask yourself, what's one step removed from that?

For example, if you usually buy pasta spirals, buy pasta tubes instead. If you usually get yellow cheddar, get a slightly orangey-coloured one for a change. If you usually cook plain pork sausages, substitute pork and apple sausages. Remember, at no time put any pressure on them to actually eat the new food.

As time goes on, you can take bigger, braver steps. Have a completely different vegetable with dinner tonight (marrow rather than broccoli), put something different on top of the pizza (parma ham instead of ordinary

ham), buy a fruit they've never tried before (a passion fruit or a coconut), choose and cook something together from the recipe book that you've never eaten before.

The paediatric dietitian says...

'More trialling of new foods really helps to reduce fussy eating. You may worry about the new food going entirely to waste, but put it in perspective. You only need to offer a tiny amount and long-term it will have a really beneficial effect.'

The jam tart tray dinner

A fun way to expose your child to new foods and encourage adventurous eating is to offer them – once in a while as a treat – a 'jam tart tray dinner' or lunch. Take a baking sheet with 12 hollows (for making jam tarts or muffins) and fill each hollow with a different food from your fridge or cupboard: cubes of cheese, cucumber slices, hummus, plain popcorn, raisins and so on. The majority can be foods that your child is familiar with, but it's a great opportunity to introduce them to two or three completely new foods.

RULE NO. 14

Don't tell them what they like and dislike

A boy, about seven or eight, was choosing a drink from a fridge in a newsagent. The mother shouted from the other side of the shop, 'Are you sure you want that one? It's strawberry flavour – you don't like strawberry.'

Another child, about three, was refusing some grapes at a picnic. But you like grapes said the father. I don't, said the child. Yes, you DO, said the father emphatically.

Another mother was talking about her daughter. I gave her dinner last night and I was so pleased because she started eating the peas straightaway. I said to her, 'I thought you didn't like peas.' She said, 'I do!' But then she didn't touch another one.

Telling or reminding our children of their likes and dislikes can only exacerbate fussy eating because it completely undermines an open, flexible and adventurous attitude towards food.

It reinforces in our child's head two lists of foods: the ones they like and the ones they don't – as if these are permanent, fixed, unchangeable things.

In reality, just because we don't like a food one day, it doesn't necessarily mean we won't enjoy it another day.

STOP! You don't like them!

You may love cheese and pickle sandwiches for example, but I bet you wouldn't want them for lunch more than two or three days in a row. Our bodies need different nutrients on different days and at different times and so we may fancy something on one occasion but not another. And even if your child doesn't like a food for a month, or a year, it doesn't necessarily mean they won't like it forever!

So if your child rejects a food, don't register and label it as one of their 'don't like' foods from that point forward. Be very careful what you say. If your child has always refused to touch lettuce and then one mealtime they reach for some, stop yourself saying *I thought you didn't like lettuce*. No good can come of that. If they want it, be quiet and let them eat it! And vice versa. If one day they don't touch something they usually wolf down, resist the urge to say *But you love that...* Maybe they just don't fancy it right now, on this day.

Also, these kinds of comments and conversations make your child less likely to touch that food the next time they see it because of the power and attention they realise it gives them. The mother in the peas story above probably thought that by saying, *I thought you didn't like peas*, the child would eat more peas to prove her wrong. But her comment actually showed how pleased she was that she was eating something she didn't normally eat. The daughter seized control immediately: *right*, she thought, *no more peas for me!*

Don't predict the future!

Don't anticipate that your child is going to be fussy before they actually have been – or at least, don't show your anticipation! Avoid saying things like 'I'm cooking beef stew for dinner and I want you to at least try it, okay?' If you are at someone else's house for a meal, don't ask what they're making and say 'Ooh, I'm not sure they'll eat that.' If your child has chosen something from a menu, don't say, 'No, I think you'd better choose something else you'll definitely eat.' Your child will pick up on all these cues and signals and probably choose to live up to them.

The paediatric dietitian says...

'How a parent reacts to a child disliking a food is key. If your child doesn't like something, simply reply 'no problem'. There should be no talk of 'likes' and 'dislikes' – keep everything 'fluid'. If your child pronounced a new word wrongly, you wouldn't stop them trying to say it again!'

RULE NO. 15

Don't hide the vegetables

They used to eat all vegetables, but now they'll only eat sweetcorn and cucumber.

This type of complaint is extremely common. Vegetables are often the biggest bugbear for a fussy eater and there are plenty of books and recipes available that tell you how to try and trick your children into eating them: sneak them into a pasta sauce; shred them finely into a casserole; smother them in cheese sauce; make a smiley face out of them on top of a home-made pizza...

These techniques may get some vegetables into our child's body, but it's only a short-term quick fix. We certainly won't be able to expect them to then wolf down a helping of courgettes or swede when they come eye to eye with them 'in the flesh'!

It is important to present vegetables boldly and proudly. We only hide and disguise stuff that is bad or unpleasant in some way – like a spot on our face or a stain on the rug.

Although our children might not think this right now, vegetables are wonderful, tasty, colourful foods of nature and this is the message we want to give them. We must also give them the opportunity to get used to their true taste and texture. Again, exposure is the first crucial step.

When we wean our children, it's common to feed them a pot of puréed carrot or puréed broccoli on its own. They taste it in its 'pure' state and eat it happily. We need to continue in this same way, presenting vegetables shamelessly, without resorting to disguises and gimmicks. That's not to say we shouldn't add vegetables to a pasta sauce or blend them into a soup – as long as we do it openly – but we need to make sure children are presented with plenty of vegetables *au naturel* too.

It doesn't matter if your child doesn't touch the vegetables – just keep putting them on their plate. Persist and be patient.

Try growing vegetables and fruit

Children are much more likely to try a vegetable or fruit if they've grown it themselves. Watching things grow is exciting and exposes them to vegetables and fruit in their natural state. Even in a very small garden, you could grow raspberries in a container or salad leaves in a planter box, for example. If you don't have a garden at all, it's still possible to grow things in pots on windowsills like tomatoes, cress, herbs or even strawberries. Let your children pick the produce directly off the plant and pop it into their mouths.

The paediatric dietitian says...

'Never lie to your child about food. It builds up mistrust. If one day your child notices that you're putting cauliflower into the mashed potato, for example, they won't eat it anymore and they won't trust you anymore. It could make them suspicious, about other foods too.'

Keep preferences as preferences

Overall, I prefer scrambled eggs to eggs cooked in other ways, but there are times when I could murder a hard-boiled egg. If there's a choice of a meat or fish dish on a menu, I'll generally go for the meat, but I'd happily go to a seafood restaurant and really enjoy it. If I was only allowed tea or coffee for the rest of my life, I'd choose tea, but I still love a cup of coffee around mid-morning.

Just like us, children have preferences. You may notice that they are generally more enthusiastic about pasta than potato – though they eat both. Or that they love sweetcorn but eat peas a little less enthusiastically. Or that chicken seems to be their favourite meat.

But we must keep in mind that these are only preferences and we must keep them that way.

The danger is, that when we notice that your child prefers ham sandwiches to cheese sandwiches, or strawberries to raspberries, we stop serving the other. As a result, preferences quickly solidify into 'will eats' and 'won't eats'.

There is a desire in us to please our children, to give them their favourite, as well as a tendency to play it safe. But if we follow their preferences, we will unnecessarily be offering them a smaller range of foods. We will narrow their palates.

So if your child prefers green apples, still buy red ones as well. If they prefer cornflakes to other cereals, don't stop giving them other types too. If their favourite sandwich is tuna, don't put it in their lunchbox every day.

That's not to say they should never have their favourite – that would be mean! But don't slip down the slippery slope of always preparing the preferences.

Don't get stuck in a rut

Do you make the same meals over and over again? It's so easy to fall into this downwards spiral. Not only is there a tendency to cook the 'reliable' meals that we know our children will eat without a fuss, we may just be too busy to put much time and thought into what we're going to cook. But before we know it, we can count the number of meals our children will eat happily on one hand. Get out of the rut. Expand the menu and spiral back upwards!

The paediatric dietitian says...

'It's not possible to offer everyone's favourite all the time and this isn't a solution. When you're feeling distraught, you might be tempted to offer your child exactly the same meal as the day before because they enjoyed it and ate it all – only to find they don't eat it this time because they're bored of it.'

RULE NO. 17

Ban words like 'yuck', 'ergh', 'I don't like this' and 'I don't want that'!

How much do you hate hearing these words? Do they make you want to scream or bang your head against the fridge? There is nothing more infuriating than when you have just cooked and presented your child with a meal and they look at it – or part of it – and come out with one of these expressions.

Ban them. Introduce a firm rule in your house that these words are absolutely not allowed to be used about food.

Yuck X
Gross X
Disgusting X

Tell your children that they can think them or say them silently in their heads if they want to. But from now on, they must say nothing negative about any food they encounter whatever they think about it.

Remind them that it's up to them whether they eat something or not. So if there's no pressure, there's no need to comment.

This ban has many benefits. Firstly, you won't be driven nuts by those words again. You could have a kind of joke with your children that at the absolute most they are allowed to say, *I'm not a big fan of X* or *I don't fancy X today* – so much easier on the ears!

Secondly, your children will not be labelling and fixing foods as 'don't like' foods – not out loud anyway, and declaring something to the world is much more powerful than doing it in your head!

Thirdly, one child saying *Yuck* won't put negative thoughts about the food into another child's head that weren't there before. Peer pressure around food is a powerful thing. A child will often stop eating a food that they enjoy because another child has expressed disgust at it.

The best time to introduce this rule isn't at the dinner table in response to children actually saying any of these expressions.

You will be too irritated to deliver the rule in a relaxed way. It could make them more likely to make negative comments because they can see it annoys you. The best time to tell them about the rule is at another time entirely, when you are nowhere near food and feeling calm.

Turn it into a sort of game or challenge: let's see if you can avoid saying these words – EVER! Not at the dinner table. Not in cafés and restaurants. Not in supermarkets. Not about other people's food. And not when they've just asked you *What's for dinner?* and you tell them!

The paediatric dietitian says...

'Sweeping statements like 'I don't like this' and 'this is horrible' promote negativity towards food. It is much better to encourage your child to think about and describe their experience of the food – its taste, texture, smell...'

Go easy on the praise

Well done! You've eaten all your dinner!

Good boy eating your beans!

Wow... haven't you done well with your lunch?

Praise can be powerful. Children can thrive on it. We praise them when they're learning how to ride a bike, trying to dress themselves, doing a good job of their homework... it encourages and motivates them. So what can possibly be wrong with giving our children lots of praise for eating?

Would you praise your child for going on a fun ride at the funfair? For playing with a new toy? Watching a favourite TV programme? Or eating a bar of chocolate? No. We praise our children to boost and reward them when they are doing something that requires effort: something that is difficult, boring or unpleasant.

Dressing yourself is hard when you're only four-years old, learning to ride a bike for the first time is tricky, mastering your seven times table is pretty painful. Eating is none of these things!

Good girl!

The reward for eating is EATING! Tasting lovely, delicious food and having that nice, satisfied feeling of a full stomach.

If we keep praising our children for eating, the message we're giving is that eating is an effort or even unpleasant. It's the very opposite to what we want to convey – that food is enjoyable, a pleasure, a wonderful part of life. Research shows that overpraising our children can reduce their interest in doing whatever it is we are praising them for: They think to themselves: *Hmmm…if mum thinks this is such a big deal, maybe I'm not supposed to like doing it.*

Not only that, constant praise is another way of showing them how much we want them to eat – handing the power over to them yet again. *If I keep praising you, you'll do it more*, we think, but it may have the very opposite effect. Have you ever praised your child for doing something and they stopped doing it? Once they sense the pressure, they may well react against it!

A word on sticker charts

Be extremely cautious about using sticker charts for eating. They're often used to reward a child for eating all their dinner or eating their vegetables, but as we have already seen, these go completely against the rules. Also, they often do more harm than good because they're used inconsistently, in fits and starts, abandoned half way through or not followed through on.

A sticker chart is most effective if you focus on a very specific area, such as tasting new foods. For example, you might use one to go with the activity on page 51 where your child chooses and tries different colour foods. But be sure to use it systematically and make any reward for collecting the stickers short-term e.g. after a week. It's also a good idea to let your child decide whether they deserve a sticker or not, to develop their own sense of achievement and judgement, rather than relying on a pat on the back from you.

The paediatric dietitian says:

'Praise after every mouthful can sound very empty and patronising. Instead, finish the meal on a positive note with something like, 'I can see you enjoyed that meal' or 'That was nice, wasn't it?''

Never stop them trying something unusual or different

A group of adults were sitting in a living room drinking wine and chatting while their children played happily. There was a bowl of crisps and a bowl of olives on the coffee table. The children came to grab a handful of crisps every so often. Then a two-year old went to take an olive. His mother immediately intervened: *No darling, you won't like that. They're for the grown-ups. Have another crisp instead.* The child made a little bit of a fuss but then gave in and took a crisp.

We often stop children trying a food because we think it's too exotic/spicy/strong/unusual for them: blue cheese, spicy curry, mussels... This goes completely and utterly against our goal for them to be adventurous and open-minded eaters.

It encourages fussiness because it teaches them all of the following things in one fell swoop:

1. *Be very cautious about trying new foods — it's better to stick to foods you are familiar with.*
2. *There are foods you definitely won't like.*
3. *There is a clear-cut line between 'adults' food' and 'children's food'.*
4. *Children should only eat bland foods.*

These are all the very opposite of what we want them to think!

In the crisps and olives story, it's easy to understand the mother's reasoning: it's a risk to let her child try an olive — he might reject it, spit it out, make a mess, waste it and be a bother. But if a child shows an interest in a food and is completely open to the idea of trying it, it's counterproductive to stop them!

So if your child wants to try a new or unusual food, always let them. If it's a very strong, spicy or 'eye-watering' food, give them the tiniest bit at first, but always let them explore. The worst case scenario – they will reject it, but it's no big deal.

Don't focus on them and hover over them as they taste it either as they will sense that you are anticipating that they won't like it and this could influence them. And if they do reject it, remember, resist the temptation to say *I didn't think you'd like it!*

The paediatric dietitian says:

'Never stop a child trying anything! If a child is interested they are already halfway to liking it. Even if you're chopping raw mushrooms and your child wants to try some, let them have a nibble – just explain that mushroom is something that tastes even better when you cook it!'

'But they love gherkins'!

You may say that despite your child being fussy, there are one or two 'exotic' foods that they love – foods that you would never have expected them to like, such as goat's cheese or smoked salmon. How can this be? Usually, it's because they were exposed to it, they liked it, and you kept giving it to them! The food is now very familiar to them – and also not associated with any pressure or battles. Remember, repeatedly exposing your child to a food increases the chance of them accepting it and enjoying it.

RULE NO. 20

Relax about table manners!

I overheard a conversation between my daughter and a five-year old girl. *Sometimes I squeeze the juice out of my strawberries into my yoghurt,* said the other child. *It's really fun but my dad gets really angry.*

We all want our children to have good table manners. We don't want them to be an embarrassment when we're eating out or at other people's houses. However, there is a tendency to rush into this too soon and too hard – to expect them to be 'mini-adults' at the dinner table at a very young age. This kind of pressure only helps to kill off adventurous eating.

If we want our children to explore food through eating it, then we have to let them explore food in other ways too – especially when they're little. Babies and toddlers naturally want to learn about the world through their senses. Just as they put toys in their mouth, they want to touch food. So when they're this age, let them stick their fingers in it, feel it, squidge it, squelch it, sniff it, see what noises it

makes… Food is, after all, sensual in more ways than taste.

Don't see it as a substitute or distraction from eating it. If we let our children do this, they are more likely to grow up loving food and having positive associations with mealtimes. If we are constantly telling them off for 'playing with their food' and getting stressed by it, we are depriving them of the pleasure of food and making mealtimes unhappier than they need to be right from the start.

Yes, it can be a messy business but it's worth it. Make it as stress-free for yourself as you can by investing in some bibs with sleeves and a wipe-clean mat to go under their highchair or chair. Then it'll only take a few minutes to clean up afterwards.

As soon as they're able to feed themselves with their hands or a spoon, let them. Don't try to keep everything neat and tidy and under control by spoon feeding them beyond when you need to. This will also avoid power struggles about how much to eat and what to eat. The best approach is always one of: *Here's your food, help yourself...*

Of course, as they get older (three, four, five-years-old), you'll need to start introducing table manners, but do it gradually and gently. Even when they're six or seven, it won't hurt if they lick the yoghurt lid, hold their knife and fork slightly incorrectly, make mountains out of their mashed potato or use a raspberry as a pretend lipstick!

Don't let your desire for them to have good table manners interfere with their enjoyment and exploration of food. In the big scheme of things, getting nutritious food inside our children through non-fussy eating is way more important than what happens on the 'outside'.

Let them experiment with odd combinations of food too if they want to. Peas in their jelly? Fine. A blob of peanut butter on their boiled egg? Go ahead and let them see what it tastes like. It all encourages a happy, positive, adventurous attitude to food.

Table manner tactics

The best time to teach table manners isn't at mealtimes at all. We don't want reprimands or negativity around food. Choose a completely different time – when no-one's hungry – and turn it into a game! Grab some knives and forks and empty plates and sit at the table or even the coffee table without food and mime eating to them. Do different things wrong, one at a time (eat with your mouth open, lick your knife, speak with your mouth full). Can they pick out what it was? Then let them have a turn. You stand much more chance of them taking notice and remembering than if you nag them while they're eating.

The paediatric dietitian says...

'It's really important to look at the sensory side of food as a whole – not just what it tastes like. Being allowed to play with food makes it more familiar to the child. It makes them feel 'safe' with it.'

Have a 'sweets day' once a week – and stick to it!

We've already talked about keeping your child's diet as savoury as possible. One of the things that makes this very difficult is that there seems to be some kind of general assumption that children should be given sweets. Almost as if it is a child's right: I call it the 'old lady syndrome' based on the image of a kind old lady who keeps sweets in her handbag and wants to give them to every child she meets as a little treat. If you try to stop her, she'll look at you as if you're cruel and say, *One little sweet. That won't do any harm.* No, one little sweet won't do any harm to their health (or their teeth), but there's no need to keep giving children sweets.

These days, children are so bombarded with sweets that they have almost ceased to be a real treat anyway: there's a packet of sweets at the end of school because it was someone's birthday, a lollipop at the end of a haircut at the hairdresser's, a chocolate bar for completing a treasure hunt... There are so many other more worthwhile ways to give children a treat – with an activity, a game, an experience, a story, or just some time and attention.

Children do not need sweets to survive or be happy! Choose one day of the week to buy your children sweets from the shop. Then stick to it with superglue! Never wobble! Never waver! Never give in to pestering!

Tell your children firmly and emphatically that there is one day when they get sweets. Friday or Saturday is the obvious choice because they have the hurray-it's-the-weekend feel. Although someone told me recently they chose Monday, *because Mondays are flippin' hard!*

If your children only have sweets on the chosen day and not randomly here and there through the week, you're going to keep their palate much more savoury, which is – as we have already talked about – vital in the battle against fussy eating. They also won't be filling up on empty calories, which will leave more appetite and room for nutritious food.

Once this rule is in place, you will no longer get pestered for sweets every time you go into a supermarket or shop. If your child knows that you

will never, ever (ever!) buy them sweets on any day but their allotted day, they really won't bother to ask. They'll quickly learn. Of course there will be parties and all sorts of other occasions and situations when sweets will crop up, but for trips to the shops, stick to the rule!

Beware: If you do ever crumble and give in, you'll make the situation much worse, because it will teach them they just have to pester harder to get what they want!

The bread roll trick

When you're shopping in the supermarket with your child, a great 'treat' to substitute for sweets is a single fresh bread roll from the bakery section. It's good because it's easy, cheap, savoury, nutritious and it'll last them quite a long time! It also gives them the fun of choosing from a wide variety (long, round, soft, crusty, white, brown, seeded...). It can actually become something they look forward to on a shopping trip!

The paediatric dietitian says...

'To avoid pestering and battles, buy treats on the day or at the time they are going to be eaten – don't buy them on a Monday and keep them in the cupboard until Friday for example! Never withhold sweet treats as a punishment as this sets up a strong emotional connection with those foods.'

RULE NO. 22

Let them eat at their own pace

Come on. Eat up!

Ooh, you're being very slow...hurry up!

Can I have that if you're not going to eat it?

My daughter is a bit like a tortoise among hares at our dinner table. The rest of us are all relatively fast eaters. She, on the other hand, eats slowly by nature, plods away at it, takes her time, takes the odd break – but still eats a substantial amount in the end. There's no doubt she loves her food.

It's all too easy to interpret slow eating as fussy, reluctant eating or to think their slowness is a sign that they don't really like the food or to assume that they're not going to eat much of it. But a slow eater is not necessarily a fussy eater – or a small eater. Some children just eat slowly!

READY! STEADY! GO!

If you have a slow eater, never rush them or push them to eat faster. Don't look at what's still untouched on their plate and tell them to eat it. Remember, any focus on what they have and haven't eaten could trigger unnecessary power struggles.

Don't be tempted to take food off their plate during the meal for yourself either, assuming they're not going to eat it. They may just have not got to it yet. They may even be saving it for last! Don't even ask them if you can have it.

Also avoid whisking their plate away too early because you assume they've finished and have eaten as much as they're going to eat. This will put pressure on them to eat faster than they naturally would. They may just be taking a break, taking their time. A slow eater could become a small eater if they don't have the chance to eat as much as they want to. Just allow a little more time for meals, especially if you need to be somewhere at a particular time.

It's important that children feel 'safe' with their food – that it's theirs to eat if they wish to and at their own pace. How would it make you feel if someone started taking food off your plate or taking your meal away before you'd finished? Twitchy? Protective? Like vultures were hovering? It's hardly a relaxing way to eat!

If everyone else in the family has finished, try to sit around and chat for a while. Eating is not a race. In fact, if anything, we want to encourage a more leisurely, social, relaxed pace of eating – not a functional gobbling down of food.

A word on serving food

A more laid-back way to eat is to copy the style of many Asian and some European countries – where instead of presenting each person with their own plate of food, you give them an empty plate and put dishes of different foods on the table. People can help themselves to the amount they want, bit by bit, going back for more as they wish until they are full. This can be done with even very 'British' meals of the meat, potato and veg kind if you want to. Investing in a rotating 'Lazy Susan' for the table could make this style of eating even more appealing to a child!

The paediatric dietitian says...

'Don't rush mealtimes. Aim for at least 30 minutes dedicated time with no interruptions or distractions. Telling your child to hurry or eat up adds extra pressure and can result in a bigger battle.'

49

RULE NO. 23

Offer the vegetables first

There is a restaurant we occasionally eat at with our children where they do something that seems a bit odd the first time you go. While you are waiting for your food to arrive, they bring you a big complimentary plate loaded with fresh, raw vegetables – and a knife: a whole lettuce, whole tomatoes, whole carrots, half a cucumber, radishes, even spring onions. Nothing else. No dressing. No dip. Just the simple, uncut veg. It sounds strange, but actually, when you're hungry and waiting for your meal, they are very, very appealing. We all attack them!

You can use this same technique at home.

If your child is anti vegetables, give them some vegetables before their main meal. Present them while you are still cooking as a sort of 'mini-starter'.

This isn't a replacement for giving vegetables with the main meal – you should still serve those too. But vegetables are going to look a lot more enticing when they're hungry and they're much more likely to eat them.

Of course, there's no need to offer them in such a simple and 'rustic' way as the restaurant, or in such big portions – and I wouldn't recommend letting them loose with a knife unsupervised!

The kind of thing you could give is:

- a handful of still frozen, ultra-crunchy sweetcorn or peas straight from the freezer in a tiny dipping bowl or egg cup
- crunchy, shredded, white cabbage with soy sauce to dip it in
- a 'kebab' of cherry tomatoes and cucumber on a stick
- carrot sticks, celery sticks, sticks of red pepper with hummus or another dip
- pickled vegetables like olives or roasted peppers with cocktail sticks (supervise with younger children)
- a small bowl of salad with a dressing.

Don't make a big thing of it. Just present the vegetables nonchalantly while they're still playing, watching TV or chatting to you. Say nothing at all or just something casual along the lines of, *Here's something to snack on while you're waiting for your dinner if you fancy it. Doesn't matter if you don't.* Just keep the servings extremely small at first. Then, whatever their response, keep doing it!

Fight the beigeness!

Chicken nuggets, white bread, cereal, crisps, chips... What do the foods that fussy eaters tend to lean towards have in common? They are all a bland, uninteresting colour...sort of beige. These foods generally contain less nutrients than a brighter, more colourful diet that includes lots of vegetables and fruit. To expose them to a wider spectrum of colour, try this activity. Each week, at the supermarket, ask them to pick a colour and then find and choose three foods of that colour that they don't normally eat. Eg. for purple: grapes, beetroot, blackcurrant jelly (allow one sweet food if they wish!).

The paediatric dietitian says...

'Offering vegetables before a meal is a great technique. Children often request snacks before mealtimes as they're hungry and don't like to be kept waiting. Offering vegetables will provide good nutrition and won't reduce their appetite like crisps or other carbohydrate foods.'

Don't use food as emotional comfort

Children are emotional creatures and as parents we have to listen to and deal with a lot of crying: they've fallen over, they're fighting with a sibling, they don't want to get in the buggy, you won't buy them that toy… It can be exhausting!

An easy, sure-fire way to stop the crying quickly in these situations is to give them something nice to eat. We might reach for a mint from our bag, give them another biscuit, open a packet of crisps or pop into

the shop for a lollipop, ice-cream or doughnut. Da-nah! It distracts them from whatever upset them, comforts them, cheers them up – and above all, stops the noise! It's peaceful again and we can swiftly move on. What a fantastic quick fix! Like an emotional band-aid.

However, giving food to our children to comfort them in this way is something we should avoid. It absolutely doesn't help in the fight against fussiness.

We are presenting food – especially sweet, fatty, salty foods – as having the power to make the world okay again. This sub-consciously trains children to turn to food when they're feeling upset or down, regardless of their body's needs – and is likely to give them a stronger leaning towards unhealthy foods.

Fussy eating aside, a tendency to seek instant, short-term comfort in food to numb the emotions could lead to overeating, even obesity, especially in the teenage years or adulthood (people rarely seek refuge in carrot and celery sticks!). Of course, the food doesn't actually deal with the emotional pain. It just suppresses it – almost like stuffing the emotions back down through the mouth rather than letting them out.

So next time your child is crying, fight the urge to 'plug' the noise with food.

Use cuddles and sympathy instead. Although it may take a little longer to quieten them down, it is a much better solution.

And for older children with a bigger or more complex issue that is upsetting them, a proper chat with some good listening is a better solution than *How about a piece of cake?* or *Let's go to McDonalds for lunch to cheer you up?*

The paediatric dietitian says...

'Don't use any food as emotional comfort - even healthy foods. And be aware that sometimes children say they're hungry when they're actually bored.'

RULE NO. 25

Be a good role model

Are you a non-fussy eater? Are you a healthy eater? How would you rate yourself out of ten on each of these accounts?

If we want our children to be happy, healthy, non-fussy eaters, we have to role model good eating. If they see us picking at our food, leaving the vegetables, saying *Ergh* or *I don't like this*, eating the same foods over and over again, regularly stuffing down crisps and chocolate bars or eating on the hoof, we have very little chance of them being different – and very little right to expect them to be!

Be brutally honest with yourself. Do you have any fussy or odd habits around food?

They may be quite subtle. Do you love food but eat it really quickly because you hate sitting at the table for long? Do you comment on the cooking at other people's houses if the meal isn't made in exactly the same way you would cook it?

Eat your veg!

Do you look at your meal when it's served and immediately pass food onto your partner's plate if there's something you don't want?

Your children will absorb everything you do around food – even if it seems as if they're not paying any attention. They will assume your bad habits are acceptable – or the norm – and there's a big chance they'll copy you.

So if you realise you do have any hang-ups or unhealthy habits around food, try to overcome them – or at least don't make them obvious in front of your children. Apply all the rules in this book to yourself too!

For example, if you're making a vegetable mini-starter for the children, make one for yourself too. Don't comment negatively about what's on your plate. Be adventurous in trying new foods. Don't have conversations about what you like and don't like. And keep your diet as savoury and nutritious as possible.

As often as possible, sit down with your children and eat the same meal together so that they see you eating and learn good habits from you. But just let it happen by osmosis. Don't draw attention to what you're doing (*Look, mummy's eating it* or *I'm going to eat all my salad – I love it*). That'll only give them something else to react against!

No 'mummy's' cupboard

Don't have a 'mummy's' or 'daddy's' cupboard or container full of goodies at home which is off-limits to your children – not even a secret one! If they discover it, it'll be a major setback. Try to eat your cakes, chocolate and sweets when you're out or at the same time as your children are having their treat.

The paediatric dietitian says...

'A powerful way to encourage a child to eat something is to model it yourself. If you never drink water, for example, then you can't complain that your children won't drink it! Self-reflection and the realisation that your children mimic your eating habits can cause feelings of guilt, but it's really important.'

Stick to 'real' food

There aren't many dishes or meals that haven't been turned into a convenience food: you can get microwavable mashed potato, chilli con carne from the chilled section, egg fried rice in a pouch, even a roast dinner in a box.

In our hectic lives it's so easy to take the easy route and go for these grab-and-heat options. What's more, we know that these foods will taste exactly the same every time, so if our children like something, they're always going to like it.

But no pain, no gain! If we really and truly want our children not to be fussy about food, we need to cook from scratch as much as possible. It really does make a difference.

Convenience foods are often enhanced with high amounts of sugar, salt and other flavourings. This makes them an instant 'hit' with the taste buds. If your child has a lot of this type of food, their palate will get accustomed to it, expect it, want it. The true taste and texture of food will seem less appealing.

These foods also severely limit children's exposure to even the sight of 'real' food. As they are simply presented with the end product, direct from the oven or microwave, they don't see the original, uncooked ingredients that go into preparing a dish. They may have no awareness that a ready-meal lasagne, for example, contains beef, tomato, onion and cheese. It goes without saying that convenience foods are generally less healthy and nutritious too.

So buy the ingredients and cook from scratch in the traditional way as much as you can. If it's been a long time since you did this – or if you're not the most confident cook – start with some really simple things. Just put a baked potato in the oven for a couple of hours and serve with grated cheese or tuna mayonnaise. Instead of grabbing a jar of pasta sauce, fry up some chopped onion, a tin of chopped tomatoes and some tomato purée. Maybe add garlic and herbs. Rather than shoving a ready-made pizza in the oven, make your own pizza dough with flour, dried yeast, salt and oil. Then put tomato purée and mozzarella cheese on top. You can get plenty of recipes from the internet or library books which will tell you how to knock up nutritious meals in the same time it takes to heat a ready-meal in the oven.

Of course, the more you cook from scratch, the easier, quicker and more automatic it becomes. Rather than fighting against it, try to enjoy the process!

The paediatric dietitian says...

'When you are reducing convenience foods, don't be tempted to try to mimic foods like chicken nuggets with your own home-made versions – you won't be able to make them taste the same! Instead, try new chicken dishes and give your children time to get used to the new flavours.'

RULE NO. 27

Make the dinner table a happy, relaxed, 'together' place to be

'Eating is a social thing in France. We chat. It's leisurely. I always looked forward to meals as a child for this reason – even when it was liver!' *(Delphine Louret, French mother)*

'The family gather together to eat and the children are pleased. Food connects people. In China, even taking a holiday together is less important than eating together!' *(Megan Wang, Chinese mother)*

Picture your dinner table in your mind. How does it make you feel? Good? Neutral? Or bad – a place you associate with battles, tension, tantrums and tears?

If it's the latter, it needs to be remedied. As we've said before, we want our dinner table to be a place of only positive associations. At the risk of sounding cheesy, it should be a happy place where the family come together to talk, catch up on each other's days, laugh and relax – while eating. Just like in a certain gravy advert!

When called to the table, our children should come with a spring in their step and a good feeling – whatever food we're serving!

Obviously, to achieve this, the first thing we need to be doing is eating together as a family. The ideal would be to eat dinner together every day, but of course this just isn't possible for many families, because of work or other commitments. But try to do it as often as you can.

Take a close look at your family routine. Where could you fit in more meals together? Could you drop or rearrange some of your children's after-school activities? Could you rejiggle your work routine at all? Could you squeeze more family meals in at the weekend? We really need to make eating together a priority for so many reasons. Studies have shown that regularly sharing sit-down meals as a family results in children who eat more fruit and vegetables, have healthier eating habits in general and are at less risk of obesity and eating disorders. The research even suggests that eating with your family improves academic achievement and emotional adjustment! Certainly, when your children are teenagers, it may be the only time you can be sure you'll coincide and communicate with them for any length of time!

Try to make meals as leisurely as possible too. We have a tendency to be quite functional about mealtimes. They should be as much about family togetherness and conversation as eating: a respite from our often busy and chaotic lives.

By following the rules in this book you will automatically be taking away the pressure on your children to eat and the battles over food. Any tensions will gradually evaporate anyway and the dinner table will become a nicer place to be.

Conversation spring-boards

You may say, but my children don't seem to want to talk at the dinner table. How was school today? you ask. Okay, they say. What did you do? you ask. Nothing, they reply. Try asking less open-ended questions, like What was the best/worst bit of school today? or How many points out of ten do you give school today – and why? If that still doesn't work, at least your child knows you showed an interest. Tell your children something about your day instead or talk to your partner – your child may well chip in and get involved. There are also many different packs of 'Conversation cards' you can buy with questions to spark off fun and interesting conversations.

The paediatric dietitian says:

'If you are in a situation where you don't have a dinner table, try and create somewhere you can sit down and eat together – with the TV off. You could lay out a blanket on the living room floor.'

RULE NO. 28

Involve them in the cooking – even if it's a hassle!

I caught a bit of the TV programme *Junior Masterchef* recently: children aged nine to 12 competing to see who was the best cook. They were jaw-droppingly good. Apart from wondering how on earth they got such sophisticated culinary skills at such a young age, I thought to myself how there wasn't even a hint of fussiness in their menu choices: spinach and ricotta ravioli, pan-fried chilli scallops, chicken liver pâté... they were about as adventurous and exploratory as you can get!

There is no doubt that involving our children in preparing and cooking food helps fight fussiness. It's a fun and stimulating thing for them to do which encourages an interest in food and a desire to try different things.

Children are much more likely to try something that they've helped you make or made themselves. And they can't cook something without getting up close to the ingredients, handling them, smelling them – so it's another way to expose them to different foods.

Of course, it may be a bit more trouble. It may be messy. It may even be irritating at times. It's always easier and quicker to do things yourself, but keep the big picture in mind. It will make a difference.

There's no need to stick to cake and biscuit-making. Even with toddlers, there's always a job they can do as you prepare a meal, from mixing and stirring, to tearing lettuce, to adding ingredients, to rinsing vegetables. Involve them in any way you can. Older children can learn to do pretty much anything you can do. Look through recipe books together, go shopping for the ingredients, try out new dishes and watch programmes like *Junior Masterchef*!

And if they want to cook something on their own – great. Don't hover and interfere unless they ask for your help. Being trusted and allowed to use their own initiative is much more motivating. Let them be inventive. Let them experiment. Put up with the chaos!

As they improve at cooking, you could let them host their own dinner party for your friends – if you're brave enough! Or you could hold a *Ready, Steady Cook!* type of family challenge in which teams have to make a meal with a random bag of ingredients that they give each other.

It doesn't matter if it works out or not. It all promotes an adventurous attitude to food!

The paediatric dietitian says...
'Cooking provides endless opportunities for tasting and experiencing new flavours. A past fussy eating patient of mine is now training to be a chef!'

RULE NO. 29

Have fun and adventures with food

Dealing with a fussy eating child can be worrying, exasperating and exhausting. It hardly puts you in a good mood!

To help blast away any black clouds of battle and angst that are hovering, we need to sometimes have light-hearted, playful, adventurous fun with food.

I'm not talking about food fights! I mean exploring food together in a way that shows it can be enjoyable and exciting – mini-adventures and challenges which reawaken their natural curiosity and interest in food. Here is a mix of ideas from quick, low-key activities to whole days out:

• Go to a farmer's market and try all the tasters on offer together, however exotic (garlic cheese, watercress soup, venison and cranberry sausage!). Give each one a mark out of ten.

• Let young children weigh and price all the vegetables and fruit you're buying on the scales in the supermarket – even if it takes up a little more time.

- Go to Pick-Your-Own farms. Try the different fruits directly off the bushes.

- Go to children's food festivals or one of the many other festivals focused on food around the UK: cheese, garlic, fish, Thai, slow food and so on.

- Grow vegetables and fruit – there are lots of small, ready-to-grow kits available if you're not the green-fingered type.

- Give your child a blindfold taste test. Prepare lots of tiny tasters (peanut butter, cheese, a piece of carrot). Pop them in their mouth one by one and see if they can guess what each food is.

- Teach them how to use chopsticks or let them eat their dinner with 'children's chopsticks' which are like tongs (you can often get these from a noodle bar).

- Surprise them with a candlelit dinner.

- Have an indoor picnic in the living room for lunch – or let them have one under the table.

- Go to different nationality restaurants. Conveyer-belt sushi restaurants are really fun – and they're not all sushi!

- Cook with your children using vegetables in bizarre, but delicious ways, like beetroot and chocolate muffins or courgette cupcakes. The idea isn't to trick them into eating vegetables but to introduce vegetables through an activity they'll find fun.

- Check out all the different types of fish at the fish counter or fishmonger with your children.

- Have 'international meal' nights at home. How about a Japanese meal sitting on the floor?

- Let your child choose a completely new food to try from the supermarket, from a different category each week (a cheese, a fruit, a soup).

- Buy a 'Lazy Susan' rotating tray for your dinner table.

There should – as always – be no pressure to eat anything. Keep it light, laugh, let the stress go. Just enjoy.

The paediatric dietitian says...

'My experience tells me that those families who put some creativity into the preparation, presentation and eating of food reduce fussy eating more quickly than those who are purely functional about it.'

RULE NO. 30

Be patient, be consistent

The approach to fussy eating in this book is effective, but it isn't instant like the wave of a magic wand. It's going to take a bit of time, focus and effort.

It's like going on a diet, giving up smoking, starting a new fitness regime, deciding to watch less telly. Changing your habits and your children's takes willpower.

So gear yourself up, put the rules in this book into action and then stick to them religiously, day in, day out.

It will pay off. As your child gets used to your new way of behaving with them around food, you will start to see them behaving in new ways too. Slowly but surely you will be able to re-programme them from fussiness to unfussiness.

Be aware that there may be relapses along the way. Your child may make several steps forward and then suddenly start to miss 'old foods' and go backwards again. If this happens, just keep calm and carry on.

Once you see things are clearly going in the right direction, don't be tempted to relax the rules and revert to old ways. This will quickly undo a lot of your good work.

Even when you get to the point where fussiness isn't really an issue anymore, don't stop following the rules. Make them permanent or fussiness will gradually creep back in.

And, if you have – or go on to have – another baby, be sure to put the rules into place right from the start to prevent them becoming a fussy eater!

A word on childcare

Be careful your child doesn't receive mixed messages from different carers. If your child is looked after by a child-minder, nursery or grandparents for example, talk to them about your approach to eating and ask them to do the same as you. Make sure your partner is fully on board too!

The paediatric dietitian says...

'The motivation and consistency of the parent is a huge factor in being successful. If a child is seven years old, it has taken seven years to develop those eating habits. It won't take seven years to reverse them but it's not going to happen overnight. Expect to see real progress after a few months.'

64